TAILS OF CANBERRA

VOLUME 2

BY INA JALIL | INA J PHOTOGRAPHY

Published in Australia by Ina J Photography

First published in Australia 2025
This edition published 2025

Copyright © Ina Jalil 2025

Cover design, typesetting: WorkingType (www.workingtype.com.au)

The right of Ina Jalil to be identified as the
Author of the Work has been asserted in accordance with the
Copyright, Designs and Patents Act 1988.

All rights reserved. No part of this publication may be reproduced, stored in a retrieval system, or transmitted, in any form or by any means without the prior written permission of the publisher, nor be otherwise circulated in any form of binding or cover other than that in which it is published and without a similar condition being imposed on the subsequent purchaser.

ISBN: 978-1-7642602-1-3

A Journey of Love and Connection

With Ina J Photography, every session is more than just taking photographs, it's about capturing the essence of your pet and the bond you share. Whether you're surrounded by nature or in the comfort of my home studio, your session is designed to be personal, relaxed, and deeply meaningful.

The works of fine-art pet photography I create are timeless and of the utmost quality, but nothing about the process (or me) is stuffy or snobby.

I keep things chill, and down-to-earth. But most importantly, each and every one of my one-of-a-kind sessions is filled with life, love and the spirit of adventure.

You're not just buying photographs; you're investing in a piece of your pet's history, a timeless tribute to a love that will never fade. The artworks we create together are designed to honour that legacy.

About the Author and Photographer

Hello, I'm Ina Jalil. I'm the photographer and heart behind Ina J Photography.

If we haven't met yet, I'm someone who believes pets change us.

They teach us how to love fully. They make our days brighter. And when they're no longer by our side, they leave behind a space that feels huge.

Photography became my way of holding on to that love.

I've been a pet photographer for almost six years now. In that time, I've had the privilege of meeting hundreds of dogs (and other pets) and their humans across Canberra. Every family, every story, every wagging tail reminds me why I do this work.

My own story began with my heart dog, Mac.
Mac taught me that photographs are more than pretty pictures.
They become anchors through grief.
They help us remember the joy that still exists beneath the heartbreak.

He passed away from heart failure at just nine years old. Far too young. But the images I took of him before he left became my comfort. They sit proudly on my walls as artwork I see every single day. They remind me of his cheeky grin, the softness in his eyes, the way he always looked for me in a room. What I wished for more of were photos of me and Mac, photos capturing our connection and bond. That is the gift I now want others to have too.

Today, my life is filled with my three beautiful dogs who each have a spot in my heart now: James, Pippa and Rosie. They keep me laughing. They keep me going on days that feel tough. And they're a big part of why I understand the families and people I photograph so well. Because I don't just document pets. I live this love every day.

With every session, my goal is simple.
To create something real.
Something you can touch and treasure.
Something that becomes part of your home and your history.

I specialise in personalised artwork because those moments deserve to be seen, not forgotten on a hard drive. Wall art, albums, portrait boxes. Pieces that add warmth to your space and make you smile every time you walk past. Every design is tailored to reflect your pet and the unique relationship you share. No two stories are the same, so no two artworks ever should be.

Beyond photography, community connection is incredibly important to me. Through projects like the Canberra Paws Pet Calendar and now *The Tails of Canberra* series, I've raised over $70,000 for local pet charities. That collective effort says so much about this city and its big-hearted pet lovers.

Tails of Canberra is a celebration of that love. A way to honour the dogs that make our lives full and help pets in need at the same time. Being part of the global Tails of the World™ Collective has shown me how powerful storytelling can be. Volume 1 of *Tails of Canberra* was an incredible journey. It was my first book. It taught me a lot, not just by meeting so many beautiful families and humans and their dogs but also about how to create a meaningful book and project. Volume 2 feels even more special as I continue building a visual record of the dogs who shape life here in our beautiful community.

Thank you for holding this book in your hands and reading these stories.

My hope is that as you turn the pages, you feel something familiar.

The excitement of a tail that can't stop moving when you walk in the door.

The comfort of knowing your dog is always close by.

You might even find yourself thinking about how you'd like to remember your own dog in the years ahead. What parts of their personality you never want to forget. What moments deserve to live on your walls and become part of your home.

Every dog in this book is deeply loved.

They are family.

And that is worth celebrating.

Here's to our dogs.

To the memories they create.

And to the love that never leaves.

**Cheers,
Ina Jalil | Ina J Photography**

About the Charity - Completely Rescued

As part of the *Tails of Canberra Volume 2* book project we raised $1,875 from the book registrations. Any profits from the sales of the book will also be donated to Completely Rescued.

Courtney Smith founded Completely Rescued, a registered charity, in 2022. The charity is driven by Courtney's deep love of animals and her commitment to creating better outcomes for pets and their families. Since inception, Completely Rescued has successfully rehomed over 350 animals, giving them a second chance at life while supporting the people who care for them. Their mission is twofold: to provide a safe pathway for animals in need and to support the community in making compassionate, informed choices about their pets.

Completely Rescued assists families who, for various personal or financial reasons, are unable to continue caring for their animals. By offering a structured and supportive surrender process, they reduce the pressure on pounds and ensure animals don't end up abandoned or neglected. Beyond rehoming, they also focus heavily on education and prevention. They provide training, guidance, and behavioural advice to pet owners who are struggling, helping them better understand their animals and avoid unnecessary surrenders. By empowering owners with knowledge and support, they are reducing the number of pets entering the rescue system in the first place.

Completely Rescued has become a vital community resource. They work closely with local councils, pounds, veterinary clinics, and other rescue groups to create strong partnerships that maximise their collective impact. The organisation is 100% volunteer driven, sustained by community donations, fundraising, and the tireless dedication of their foster carers and supporters. While their heart is in saving animals, their vision extends to strengthening the bond between people and their pets, alleviating stress for families, and building a more compassionate community. Every animal they help represents not only a life saved but also hope and reassurance for the people who love them.

What began as one woman's mission to fill a gap in the rescue system has grown into a movement built on empathy, teamwork, and education. Courtney saw first-hand how overwhelmed pounds were and how many families simply needed a helping hand rather than judgment. Completely Rescued bridges that gap-offering understanding, solutions, and a second chance. Every rescue, from the timid kitten learning trust to the senior dog finding peace in their golden years, tells a story of resilience. These stories inspire others to foster, adopt, and give back. Through every act of care, Completely Rescued continues to remind the community that kindness has the power to change lives–both animal and human alike.

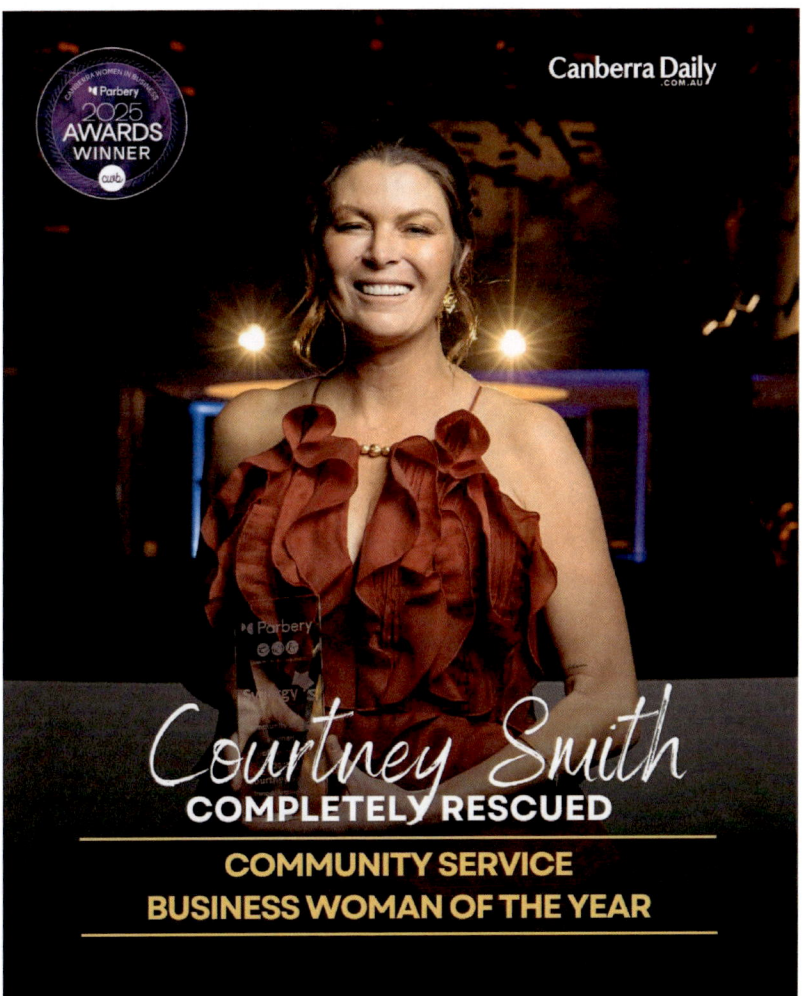

"A dog is the only thing on earth that loves you more than they love themself."

Josh Billings

life. love. adventure

Contents

A Journey of Love and Connection	v
About the Author and Photographer	vi
About the Charity - Completely Rescued	viii
Jellyfish and Clyde	1
Harry	2
Mia and Addie	5
Lulu and Bailey	7
Peggy	8
Phoenix	11
Gretel	13
Peggy	14
Macgyver	16
Hendricks and Penny	19
Darcy and Kacchi	21
Lenny and Myra	22
Yuki	24
Bonnie and Arli	26
Harley and Rosie	29
Maya	31
Gidget	32
Harris	34
Polly-Pocket	37
Laila	39
Scout	40
Hank	42
Xena	45
Rama	47
Ivy, Dixie, Jasper and Bottas	48
Griffin, Womble, Morrigan, Frenix and Rorschach	50
Thankyou to our sponsors	53
Your Dog's Story. Your Home. Your Heart.	62

Jellyfish and Clyde

Dear Jellyfish and Clyde,

Jellyfish, your blindness has never stopped you from showing me your beautiful personality and making me laugh every day. I've woken up to new artwork on the walls and couches, I even lost some underwear to your teeth!

I've never had a dog with this much energy before; you've opened up a whole new world for me. From dog sports to hikes, nosework classes and running ... we've had so many adventures together and proved many people wrong along the way.

It sometimes makes me sad to think that you will never know what I look like, or how beautiful the sunrise is and the waves at the beach. I think this is a very human worry, because you love life so much, I don't think you'd be able to love it more if you had sight. I'm inspired by you every single day, and so lucky to have you in my family. 🖤

Clyde, you jumped headfirst into our lives and took on your new baby brother so easily, it's like you were meant to be with us.

I didn't realise at first just how much people in your past have broken your trust, and I always wondered how you escaped them. You spent so long roaming the Queensland bush on your own; you even got seriously injured on the way. I'm forever thankful to the person who found you, and the rescuers who healed you and brought you to me.

I've loved watching you build trust with my family, and push yourself in classes and on our adventures. You don't let your past dictate your future, and I'm so proud of you for that. 🖤

Love,
Anastasia and Harley

Harry

To our Wonder Dog, Harry

From the moment I first saw you as a tiny puppy playing with your brothers and sisters, you stood out. That adorable look of yours is still so vivid in my memory, and even now, eleven years later, you haven't changed. You're still that same excited boy, always ready for an adventure.

When Heidi came into your life four years ago, it felt as though she had known you forever. She once thought only big dogs could make a big impact, but you've shown her just how wrong that was. You've filled both our lives with love, joy, fun, and laughter (and just enough cheekiness to keep us on our toes).

Your love for chicken nuggets is as unwavering as your love for us, and our love for you is greater than you will ever know. You are our best boy, our companion, and our heart.

**With all our love,
Andreas and Heidi**

Mia and Addie

To our dearest Mia and Addie,

Where do we even begin? You both hold the most precious parts of our hearts, each in your own unique and wonderful way. Our lives are infinitely richer because of you, and there isn't a single day that goes by where we don't feel grateful for the joy, chaos, and love you bring into our world.

Mia, our soul dog, our first fur baby, you changed our world the moment you bounded into it. Your big brown eyes and cheeky personality brought light to the long days and comfort on the lonely nights. Through every posting, from Darwin to Wodonga to Puckapunyal, and finally back to Canberra, you have been our home. No matter where we were, as long as we had you, we were never alone. You have a gift– an unexplainable ability to win over every person you meet. You're our safe place. Our family. Our heart dog. The thought of life without you is one we cannot bear, but we promise to cherish every single moment we have left together.

And Addie, you're our wild child, our chaos queen, our beloved doofus. If Mia is our heart, you are our laughter. You burst into our lives like a whirlwind, turning our quiet world upside down with your boundless energy and unstoppable need for attention. You were meant to be the contingency plan, but instead you became the biggest surprise of all. Life with you is chaotic, messy, and full of love, and we wouldn't have it any other way.

Together, you two have shaped our lives in ways we never could have imagined. You've shared in our joys and held us through our sorrows. You are our family, our babies, and our greatest blessings. We are so incredibly proud to share your stories through *Tails of Canberra*. It means the world to us to have this moment captured forever. No matter what the future holds, you will always be our girls, our hearts, and the greatest joys of our lives.

**With all our love, forever and always,
Your hoomans, Ayla and Brendan**

Lulu and Bailey

Dear Lulu and Bailey,

How lucky I am to have you both in my life; you are the loves of my life and my world.

Lulu, you have been with me for 10 years and we have shared many highs and lows together. When you were so sick and I wasn't sure that you were going to survive, you showed your true fighting spirit and amazed me with your strength to rally and recover. I treasure every day that we get to spend together. I love your quirky ways, especially your love of licking the furniture which always make me laugh. Even though you have an independent spirit, you are still happy to snuggle up next to me and let me give you cuddles.

Bailey, my crazy boy, you have been with me for 16 months and there is never a dull moment with you in my life. Our walks are always fun because you love exploring new areas and meeting new people. There is nothing better than coming home and you're at the gate with that beautiful look on your face that I have come back to you. My favourite time of the day is when you snuggle up next to me at night when we go to bed.

Thank you, Lulu and Bailey, for the unconditional love you give to me and for filling my days with so much joy and happiness.

**With all my love,
Bernie**

Peggy

My sweet little Peggy,

In this life, you're meant to have one great dog.

One that shifts something deep inside you in a way you never see coming. You are that dog for me. You came into my life at the best of times and filled it with so much joy. Even in the smallest, most ordinary moments, you've changed me.

I think of all the nights I've been woken by your little snores, adorable snores that put a smile on my face every time, even when it's 2.00 am.

You make life so much more meaningful. You're my anchor, the one who steadies me when I'm teetering on the edge. Just by being there, you've shown me a kind of love I didn't think existed.

And that's the thing about having one great dog, you make me wonder how I ever lived before you. When I look at you lying there, I know you've given me more than any person ever has. Your presence says, "I'm here, always with you", and that's changed everything.

No other creature, human or otherwise, has made such a wonderful impact on my life. You are the epitome of kind, wrapped in silly, sweet fun, and a loyal, loving friend.

Peggy, my soul dog. My now and forever love, Dhuse

Phoenix

Dear Phoenix,

I loved you from the moment I saw you. Your photo jumped out at me straight away from all the other puppy photos.

You came into our house to help us heal and that you did. You immediately brightened up my life and have warmed my heart every single day since. You never fail to make me smile; you are my comfort, and the best gardening buddy ever.

I love the little tail flick you do when you are falling asleep. The way you cuddle me like a fluffy meerkat when I come home. The way you stalk your ball and chase leaves. The way you are always enthusiastic and ready to be involved in whatever I am doing but also happy to just sit and chill with me. I love your spark for life, your zest for play and your love of tummy wubs and, of course, food!

**Thank you for being in my life, Miss Phoe,
Cheryl**

Gretel

To my girl, G,

You came into my life about two-and-a-half years ago after a friend sent me a Facebook post. In true Canberra fashion, I had crossed paths with your owner through work; I took it as a sign that you were meant to come into my life.

You're sweet and smart but my god do you come with some sass. I suppose I should take it as a compliment though; they say dogs take after their owners. Your excited little tippy taps as you wait for your ball, your tail wagging so hard I'm surprised you haven't hurt yourself and your smile that looks like a snarl are your little quirks that make you so loved.

We have so many memories together but my favourite is probably from our first few weeks together. We went down to Lindsay Pryor National Arboretum. It was autumn and the leaves were red, orange and purple. We just walked and I threw the ball. It was peaceful and the first time I felt that you were truly mine. We ended up choosing the same location for our photoshoot and having that memory and connection; it just made the location all the more special.

You're my soul dog and I'm so glad that I get the chance to share you with everyone with this book.

**Love,
Courtney**

Peggy

My dearest Peggy,

From the moment I saw your photo on Facebook, I knew I had to adopt you. Since that day, the world has felt immeasurably brighter with you in it.

Thank you for the little things:

- The way you stand like a curious little meerkat, head tilted and eyes wide–always alert, full of wonder–that sight never fails to make me smile.

- Your love for playing in the water, no matter the weather–whether it's a drizzle or a downpour, you're splashing with joy.

- Curling up beside me while I watch TV–nestled in my lap, softly sighing as you rest your head–a quiet lesson in love's simplicity.

You are pure sunshine–playful, affectionate, radiant. Everyone who meets you feels that spark of joy you carry so effortlessly. You continually remind me that happiness exists in the simplest of moments: a walk, a wag, a warm cuddle on a cold night.

You've changed my world. You've taught me patience, laughter, and the beauty of quiet companionship.

**With all my love, always,
Cara**

Macgyver

Dear Mac,

If you could understand one thing it would be how much we love you even when you are being a complete ratbag. You bounded into our lives, all paws and mischief; you kept us on our toes, rearranging cushions, stealing shoes and claiming the armchair as your own personal throne. But through all this chaos you have given us joy, purpose and healing. You have encouraged Dad to get up and walk every day. Sometimes twice! He has never been healthier. So even if you don't understand our words we hope you feel our love in every pat and every treat and every time we let you steal the majority of the bed. You are our boy, our chaos and most importantly our heart. We may not have as much time with you as we imagined but we will cherish every minute.

**Love,
Duncan and Julia**

Hendricks and Penny

Hendricks and Penny,

You are everything to me and bring me so much joy! I love sharing my life with you and couldn't ask for better companions.

It was with great anticipation that Hendricks entered my life, as at 30, I'd finally settled in one location and could finally get a dog. Then I met you, Hendricks, and even all my expectations couldn't live up to the love and the joy you brought me! You changed my life in the most amazing ways, and have been my shadow, best friend and rock for the past four years. You have an old soul, a cheeky personality and so much loyalty; I just love you.

Penny, you entered mine and Hendricks' life as one of my foster dogs at just four months old. Within hours, I knew you fit perfectly into our lives and just brought endless more joy, energy and happiness to both me and Hendricks. You are my crazy little princess, ball of energy, who loves to chase the ball, play with her friends and lead her sister (who was adopted by my friends) into trouble.

Our lives together are full of fun and adventure, whether it is our morning walks which bring me a kind of joy and peace like nothing else in this world, or our trips to the beach, river, camping or just puppy play dates hanging with our other labrador friends.

Hendricks, with your eyes that can pierce into any souls to demand treats or belly rubs at any time, and to Penny, with your sass and mischief. I promise you I will continue to love and dote on you both for the rest of your lives, may they be long and happy!

**Love,
Ellie**

Darcy and Kacchi

My dearest Darcy and Kacchi,

From the moment you both entered my life, you brought endless joy, laughter, and just the right amount of mischief. Life is so much richer with you by my side.

Darcy, my chatty boy, you've never been one to keep your opinions to yourself. Whether it's demanding attention, announcing your presence to the world, or grumbling when Kacchi steals the spotlight, you always make sure you're heard. You weren't too keen on sharing your space at first, but deep down, I see how much you've come to love your little brother–even if you pretend otherwise. You are my steady, expressive, and endlessly loyal companion.

Kacchi, my little whirlwind, you burst into our lives with playful energy and a heart full of love. Your name suits you perfectly–not just because your golden fur looks like a bowl of Kacchi Biryani, but because you bring warmth, comfort, and a little bit of spice wherever you go. You make everything more exciting, and I love watching you and Darcy figure out your brotherly bond–him pretending to be grumpy while secretly adoring you.

If you could understand every word, I'd tell you this: You are my heart in two very different but equally perfect forms. You make my world brighter, my home cosier, and my life infinitely better. Thank you for every wag, every cuddle, and every moment of unconditional love. Life with you both is the greatest adventure.

**Forever and always,
Emilie**

Lenny and Myra

Lenny and Myra,

You are the dogs I didn't know I needed.

You came to me as foster dogs from Bull Arab Australia, not long after I lost my soul dog, Mac, to lung cancer. I had nursed Mac for almost three months before I lost him a week before his sixth birthday. Also a rescue, he and I were tightly bonded; we had almost three beautiful years together and it wasn't nearly long enough.

Although I knew I would have dogs in my future – Mac and I had discussed it – I wasn't sure when I would be ready to accept a new dog and as Mac had been fostered I volunteered to do the same for another dog in need.

Then into my home and heart you wandered–a bonded pair, bull arab crosses, most likely siblings, with few social skills. This was not the plan.

You had already come a long way with your first foster family, Mel and Rob, who gave you a safe home out of the pound and started the process of taking you from shut down to the confident dogs you are today. It takes a village to raise a rescue dog.

My Lenny, my big sweetheart. Lennybennyratbag boy, you put on such a brave face, with your Snoopy dog smile and those lovely brown eyes. You will stand between Myra and me and danger, real or imagined. You will randomly freak out about an object you have passed a million times without noticing and you can't start the day without belly rubs. Your FOMO is the stuff of legend, and nothing occurs in our home without your nose being firmly inserted into it.

My Myra, MyMy girl, you have slowly but surely come out of your shell. Lenny and I would have no idea where we were going on walks if we didn't have your nose to guide us. You love nothing more than hunting down a scent, galloping around the backyard running rings around your brother and when you choose me to lay your head on or snuggle up with, it's a precious gift of trust. I'm so proud of how sassy and brave you have become.

I lost a few things–there's no grass in my backyard any longer and the couch has a few bite marks taken out of it, but the richness of being part of this pack is worth those small sacrifices.

I didn't know I needed you, but I am so glad you needed me and now we have each other.

Love, Frith

Yuki

Dear Yuki,

From the day we brought you home, I vowed to give you the best life I could. We were uncertain as we were new to everything, yet you made it easy. From your first night, you were calm and kind, and we fell asleep grateful for the good girl beside us.

As you grew, you kept surprising us. We gladly "work" for you each evening with your massages, complete with the little tools we brought back from Japan. We give our Sundays to obedience school so you can serve others as a support therapy dog, a role that remains one of the proudest moments of my life. And because you deserve only what keeps you well, we bake your treats at home, carefully chosen for your allergies and full of the best nourishment.

You filled our days with joy and shared that joy with everyone you met. You are our small, steady source of joy, radiating warmth to everyone you meet. I could boast about you forever, but what I most want you to know is this: you are my daily reminder of gentleness and grace.

Most of all, thank you for choosing us.

**With all our love,
Janice and Tam**

Bonnie and Arli

Dear Arli and Bonnie,

Arli, you came into my life at a time when I really needed you. I found you on Gumtree, just a playful little boxer pup in Maitland, and from the moment I saw you, I knew you were mine. You were so sweet with Milly, my parents' old bichon cross poodle, even as you quickly grew much bigger than her. I'll never forget how you'd climb onto the table in the backyard just to watch the cars and people go by, happily greeting anyone who stopped to say hello.

The bond you shared with my dad was something truly special. He would walk you for hours every day, taking you to the shops, sitting with you on benches, even riding the lift together at Bunnings because you were scared of the escalator. The last time he held your lead, even after he had fallen and couldn't speak, showed just how strong that connection was. You remind me of him every day, and I am so grateful you shared that love together.

Then Kyle, my partner came into our lives when you were two. Our very first date was a dog playdate with you and his family dog, Koda, and it couldn't have gone more perfectly. Since then, you and Kyle have been inseparable. You play hide and seek, sleep together at night, and go on countless walks. You are our shadow, always close by, loving us unconditionally. You were my first baby, and I couldn't love you more. Your little tongue poking out when you sleep and your bum wiggles when you're excited melt my heart every time.

And Bonnie, you came to us as the most precious birthday present from Kyle. We had been dreaming of a second dog, and when we saw you and your sister at the Queanbeyan pound, we knew we had to meet you. You were nervous but sweet, and when Arli met you, it just felt right. Fate chose you that day. You were so tiny, only eight weeks old, and had been through such a rough start. But from the very beginning you were so loving, and you changed all our lives forever.

You've kept Arli young, always encouraging him to play, and you love us with all your heart. You curl up at our feet, cuddle into us, and protect me fiercely when Kyle is away. You're so clever, learning tricks so quickly, and so full of personality–whether it's splashing like a crocodile in the water, or destroying squeaky toys (except that one little mouse you've kept safe). Your happy wiggles when we come home always make us smile.

Arli and Bonnie, you are our family. Our hearts are so full because of you, and we love you more than words can say.

**All our love,
Jenna and Kyle**

Harley and Rosie

Dear Harley and Rosie,

From the moment you both came into my life, you've been so much more than just pets–you're my family, my companions, and my best mates. Harley, you were the first dog I ever called my own, and I couldn't have asked for a better one. Rosie, you may be small, but you've brought a whole lot of spark into our world with your spunk and quirks. Together, you've filled my days with joy, laughter, and love.

Harley, your personality shines in everything you do. Your obsession with fetch is unmatched; I swear you'd play all day if you could. The way you sing when I scratch that perfect spot, or how you always find a way to nudge in for a cuddle makes it impossible not to smile. You hate being too far from your favourite people, and honestly, we wouldn't have it any other way.

Rosie, you're proof that big spirit comes in a tiny package. You never forget a thing, like where a bird might have been one time, and you make sure we all know about it. Your funny little quirks keep us laughing, and when you're not on the go, you're the champion of naps, switching between either on or off, zero to one hundred and back again. And of course, your love of cuddles and belly rubs makes you the sweetest little lady.

Having you both by my side has meant everything. Harley, you've been my constant for so many years, and Rosie, you've added a whole new layer of joy to our lives. I wouldn't trade a second of it for anything. You're the best pair I could ever hope for, and I hope you both know just how deeply loved you are.

Jessica

Maya

Dear Maya,

You are pure joy and confidence wherever you go. You love to say hi to everyone we meet, always winning hearts with your friendly nature. One of our favourite things about you is your big, happy smile that melts our hearts every single time. You're incredibly smart, full of energy, and you never fail to brighten our days. We're so lucky to share our lives with you.

**With all our love,
V and JP**

Gidget

Dear Gidget,

You are pure joy. You have made us the happiest pawrents. We love every little thing about you. Your cheeky smile, your endless energy, your warm cuddles and the enthusiasm and love you gift us every day. There isn't a feeling like it.

We love you so much. You are the best pupper ever and we are so lucky to have you.

Love
Mummy and Bean xx

Harris

Dear Harris,

You came into my life when I needed a pick-me-up and have kept me up ever since. You are so cheeky, crazy and the biggest goofball. You make me laugh every day with your silly games.

The games of chase and fetch, the gleam of naughtiness in your eyes when I catch you doing something you shouldn't put a smile on my face every day.

I'm so grateful you came into my life.

I will love you forever,
Laura

Polly

Dear Polly-Pocket,

I knew you were perfect the first time I saw your picture at two weeks old with your little curly tail. I had the pick of the litter and I was drawn to you instantly. I got to bring you home when you were eight weeks old and you brought unconditional love into my life from day one.
I love how goofy you are, how one minute you are so pretty and quiet and the next you are zooming around inelegantly, making me laugh with your legs everywhere. You make the funniest faces, check in on me all the time and even though you only weigh three kilos you protect me from all harm you perceive. You are the best life companion I could have ever hoped for and I would take ten years off my life to add ten years to yours.

You're forever a piece of my heart–my Precious Princess, my Pretty Polly-Pocket, my Perfect Pick of the litter!

Love,
Linda

Laila

Dearest Laila,

You are a dream come true for me! I wish I was the person you deserve!

You fill my heart with joy every time I see you and I love how you make me more active!

I love it when you snuggle me in your sleep and roll over for a belly rub when you're barely awake!

I love how your security place is my left shoulder; I will always have a shoulder for you, my baby girl!

Thanks for choosing me to be your humum!

Love you always and forever,

**Mamma
Xoxo**

Scout

Dear Scout,

From the moment you came into our lives you have brought us so much laughter and love, and even a little bit of pain ... remember the time that Mum fell over when she was doing zoomies with you in the backyard and broke a rib?

We love that you always join us for family movie night, even though you usually sleep through the entire film. We love your magnificent floofy ears and that everyone always says, "Look at her beautiful eyelashes!". We love that you can do nothing but sleep all day yet still let out the biggest sighs and grumbles because life is oh so hard. We love your thousand-mile-an-hour zoomies that come out of nowhere and the way you jump up and throw yourself on the couch to stop. We love your constant snuggles and that you're the perfect nap buddy. We love that you're always there to supervise us to make sure the job, whatever it is, is done right. We love that you're a sucker for belly rubs and we're suckers for giving them to you. We love that you protect us from the loud bangs with equally loud barks. We love taking you out with us any chance we get because you're such a happy, friendly, social butterfly and everyone who meets you falls in love with you immediately.

You are the heart of our little family. Thank you for being the best furry friend we could ever ask for. We adore you, Scouty, little Miss Breakfast Club, our baby chicken.

**Love,
Mum and Dad**

Hank

Hank,

From the moment I saw your giant paws and expressive soulful eyes I knew that you were the one for me. You might be big, but your personality is even bigger!

Every day with you is like having a big hairy shadow that is always just one foot away. Your goofy antics and funny smiling face are the best parts of my day.

I love how you greet me and your tail that wags so hard it knocks things off the coffee table, how you sleep on your back with your legs in the air taking up the whole couch, how you lean against me pinning me against the furniture.

And let's not forget your absolute favourite thing in the world: your squeaky reindeer toy! Watching your crazy zoomies and hearing that squeaky toy echo through the house always makes me smile.

Thank you for being my giant cuddly co-worker, my buddy, and my all-time favourite pal. You're not just a dog; you're my family.

With lots of love and belly rubs,
Nicole

Xena

Xena,

You came home on a Sunday afternoon when I was 18 - a tiny, wrinkly ball of puppy breath and needle teeth. You were so quiet and calm, I was worried something was wrong. Once you settled in, though, the little velociraptor inside you emerged. You loved chewing your toys and snacks, but miraculously only ever chewed one or two shoes. Though my desk still has your tiny teeth marks from when I thought you were asleep in my lap, but you had found a lovely form of quiet entertainment. Now, you're eight years old. Watching you grow up and blossom into such a wonderful dog has been the biggest pleasure of my life. Your face is sugar-dusted now, but you will always be that tiny, wrinkly baby to me.

For eight years you've been my constant companion. There through the start and end of my first serious relationship, the loss of my grandad, starting (and dropping out of) university, the years where I didn't know what I wanted to do with my life, and then as I started my study to be a vet nurse. You were a wonderful sport, letting me practise bandaging, taking vital signs, and the myriad of other things I was learning to do. Now, you're the perfect little "patient" when something is needed at work. Happy to lie on your back for a vet to practise ultrasounds, and even saving the lives of other dogs by donating blood four times.

You may not be the perfect dog, or the best behaved, or know the most tricks, but that doesn't matter to me. You are the perfect dog for me. You've been there to dry my tears with your fur, you've made me laugh more times than I can count, and most of all you gave me a reason to keep on going when life felt like too much. I can't put into words how much I love you, or how proud I feel to be your human. You are my heart on four legs, and I promise to love you and treat you with the utmost care and dignity as you enter your golden years. I'm not lost on the fact that it is a privilege to watch you grow old-one so many others don't get with their dogs-but I wish time would slow down a little, and that you would be by my side forever.

I'll love you forever, munchkin.
Mumma

Rama

Dearest Rama,

From the moment Vanessa placed you in our arms, we knew our lives would never be the same. How could such a small bundle of fur transform our entire world? Yet you did, with your wagging tail that turns our house into a home each time we walk through the door.

Every day, we find ourselves smiling at the silliest things you do. The way you wrestle with your snake toy–pouncing on it with such determination, tossing it in the air and catching it with that look of absolute pride on your face–fills our hearts with pure joy. Such a simple pleasure, yet it brings us all such happiness.

We cherish every memory we've created together, but nothing quite compares to our swimming adventures at Currumbin Creek, Palm Beach on the Gold Coast. Watching you bound through the shallow waters, your ears flopping with each splash, your eyes alight with excitement–these are the moments we hold closest to our hearts.

We adore how you've turned people-watching on the beach into an art form. The way you sit so contentedly, observing everyone who passes by with that curious tilt of your head. And who could forget your hilarious habit of burying your head in the sand? That moment when all we can see is your wagging tail and backside while your head disappears completely–it never fails to make us laugh, no matter how many times you do it.

You are, without doubt, the most headstrong dog we've ever known–stubborn in the most endearing way. Your charm is undeniable; a true people person who draws everyone in with your irresistible personality. It's no surprise you prefer human company over other dogs–with one notable exception: your boyfriend, Billy. The special bond you and Billy share warms our hearts.

The way you seek attention, Rama, nudging hands for pets and positioning yourself at the centre of every gathering, makes it impossible not to adore you. Your love of company–particularly human, save for your beloved Billy–speaks to your beautiful, sociable soul.

You've brought immeasurable happiness into our lives. You've taught us patience, unconditional love, and how to live in the moment. Your unwavering loyalty has been our comfort through difficult times, and your joyful spirit has brightened our darkest days. You may not understand the words "forever" or "always", but we hope you feel it in every scratch behind your ears, every treat sneaked under the table, and every cuddle as we drift off to sleep.

You are loved beyond measure, Rama, not just for what you bring to our lives, but for exactly who you are–our perfect, wonderful companion.

All our love, Shinta and Damon

Ivy, Dixie, Jasper and Bottas

Ivy, Dixie, Jasper and Bottas,

Jasper, you were our very first toy poodle back in 2013, and it was love at first sight. You've always been quirky and funny, and even though you're slowing down now, you still make sure everyone knows you're "top dog" in the pack.

Dixie, you are our sweet, gentle little one, always happy to wait patiently until the perfect moment to curl up on a lap and soak up some attention.

Bottas, you keep us laughing with your boundless energy, racing through the house and garden, especially when Ivy is by your side.

And Ivy, you may be the newest addition, with a little schnauzer sparkle mixed in, but you've settled in beautifully since we adopted you last year. You've made your presence felt from the very beginning, and you bring so much fun and energy to the pack.

Minette, you're not in the picture as sadly you're no longer with us, but we feel your presence every day and you'll always be part of our poodle family.

Each of you has such a different personality, and it can be a challenge making sure you all get along–but we wouldn't change it for the world. We love you all dearly, and we can't imagine our lives without our poodle crew.

**Love,
Julia**

Griffin, Womble, Morrigan, Frenix and Rorschach

Dear Griffin, Womble, Morrigan, Frenix and Rorschach,

At almost seven years old, a stage 5 IVDD survivor and head of the pack, Grif, you lead them with a level head, a penchant for pats and tummy rubs and the calm demeanour of a wise and wily gentleman far older than your years. As a certified emotional support animal, you provide a calming influence and induce smiles to all who meet you on our journeys around Canberra, either in your wheels or in your pram.

Our Fabio-esque pretty boy, Womble, you are truly a sight to behold. We've often spotted you posing outside in the sunshine, letting your long hair waft in the breeze as the rays hit you just so. You're always ready for your close-up! You also make us chuckle and give us heart attacks when you randomly do a trust fall from the couch or our lap; we're just meant to catch you. You know we will.

Middle of the pack and our only girl, Morrigan, you're our fiery, spirited tiny bundle of energy. True to your Irish namesake (Celtic Goddess of death, war and destruction), you identify as a Great Dane trapped within your small red-haired body. You are absolutely the boss and you're only too happy to tell the world. Loudly!

Chocolate and tan, Frenix, it's almost your 4th birthday! You're our most recent addition to the pack, still finding your way and letting your personality come through. We love how you love to play with toys and keep your eyes on those pesky birds. They best be careful; you're true to your name (lightning destroyer) if the birds don't escape fast enough.

As the biggest, yet the youngest of our pack, Rorschach (Rory for short), you truly believe you're a tiny mini dachshund, not a harlequin Great Dane. Your quirky ears are a physical manifestation of your adorably derpy and goofy nature. At over 60kg, you're definitely a lap dog; if you fit, you sit!

The pack as a whole brings so much love and laughter to our lives and those friends and family who share you with us. We wouldn't trade you in for anything.

**Cheers,
Cas and Ed**

BEST IN SHOW SPONSOR

Central Bark Pet Styling: Where Compassion Meets Craftsmanship

In 2019, in a modest little premises in Gungahlin, a dream came to life. That dream belonged to Debbie Hart, a woman with a lifelong passion for working with animals and a vision to change the way dog grooming was done in Canberra. From the very beginning, Central Bark Pet Styling was more than just a business—it was a sanctuary where dogs could feel safe, comfortable, and cared for, while receiving world-class grooming services.

Operating out of that tiny space, Debbie and her team built their reputation the old-fashioned way: through hard work, genuine care, and an unwavering commitment to excellence. Clients quickly came to know Central Bark as a place where every dog was treated as an individual, where nervous pets were met with patience and kindness, and where the standard of grooming was consistently exceptional.

A Move to Match the Mission

By early 2024, it was clear that Central Bark had outgrown its Gungahlin home. The demand for appointments was soaring, and the team needed a larger, purpose-built space to meet the needs of both clients and their furry companions.

The move to Mitchell marked a turning point. The new premises offered not just more room, but also the chance to create an environment truly designed for the comfort and well-being of the animals. Every detail—from the bright, airy interiors to the thoughtfully designed grooming stations—was chosen to reduce stress and make the experience as positive as possible for each dog that walked through the door.

National Recognition

In July 2024, Central Bark reached a milestone that would put it firmly in the national spotlight. That month, the business was named Australian Women's Small Business Champion for Pet Services—a prestigious accolade awarded to a business that demonstrates outstanding service, innovation, and contribution to its community.

For Debbie, standing on that stage and accepting the award was a moment of validation—not just for her, but for every member of her team. It was proof that their hard work, attention to detail, and compassion had made an impact that extended well beyond Canberra.

A Heart for Rescue Dogs and Holistic Care

While the awards and the expansion were remarkable achievements, Debbie's philosophy has always been about giving back. Central Bark works closely with the RSPCA, offering free grooming services whenever rescue animals need them. These aren't just cosmetic transformations—grooming can mean the difference between a dog being overlooked or catching the eye of a potential new owner.

Central Bark's policy is clear and heartfelt: every rescue dog is entitled to their first groom free of charge. No exceptions, no paperwork, no questions—just a warm welcome and a transformation that helps them start their new life with dignity, comfort, and a touch of style.

Beyond grooming, the team regularly consults with dog owners, offering free advice on coat care, skin health, and general wellbeing whenever asked. Every dog is given a thorough head-to-tail check during their groom, and if anything unusual is found—such as lumps, skin irritations, ear infections, or dental concerns—the owner is immediately informed so they can seek the attention of a veterinary professional.

To ensure the highest standard of care in all situations, every staff member holds a pet first aid qualification, providing peace of mind that dogs are in capable and knowledgeable hands at all times.

The Relentless Pursuit of Excellence

Despite the accolades, Central Bark never stops striving to be better. Debbie and her team are committed to continuous learning, regularly attending national and international seminars to stay at the forefront of grooming techniques and animal care standards.

The Mitchell salon often plays host to workshops run by world-class groomers, bringing leading industry experts to Canberra so local pets—and their owners—can benefit from the very best in the business. These events aren't just about skills—they're about inspiration, sharing knowledge, and raising the bar for pet grooming across the region.

Central Bark's groomers also put their abilities to the test in competitive grooming competitions, where precision, creativity, and technical mastery are on display for expert judges. These contests push the team to refine their craft, learn new styles, and showcase the exceptional talent that has become synonymous with the Central Bark name.

At the heart of all this growth and ambition is Debbie Hart. Her leadership is defined by unwavering support for her staff, empowering them to develop their skills, express their artistry, and take pride in their work. She understands that the best results come from a team that feels valued, motivated, and passionate about what they do.

"To ensure the highest standard of care in all situations, every staff member holds a pet first aid qualification."

Website: centralbarkpetstyling.com.au
Instagram: @central_bark_pet_styling
Facebook: www.facebook.com/CentralBarkPetStyling
Address: 5/26 Sandford Street, Mitchell, ACT
Contact details: 0410 467 850
02 6174 4203

A Community Institution

Today, Central Bark Pet Styling is more than just a grooming salon—it's a trusted name in Canberra's pet care community. It's the place where first-time puppy owners come for advice, where senior dogs receive gentle, understanding care, and where rescue animals find a helping hand on their journey to a forever home.

Central Bark has a long affiliation with Ina J Photography and is honoured to be a major sponsor of the second Tails of Canberra book—an initiative that celebrates the special bond between pets and their families while raising funds and awareness for animal welfare causes.

From its humble beginnings in Gungahlin to its award-winning status in Mitchell, the Central Bark story is one of vision, persistence, and love for animals. And if the past is anything to go by, the future will hold even greater achievements —always grounded in the same core belief: that every dog deserves to look and feel their best.

"The Central Bark story is one of vision, persistence, and love for animals"

ELITE SPONSOR

Picking up poop is probably the only thing not to love about dogs!

While most dog walkers want to do the right thing and clean up after their furry friends when out in public places, it's not pleasant carrying around smelly plastic bags until you can find a rubbish bin.

Enter the Pupoon, a lightweight, airtight capsule with built-in bag dispenser that attaches seamlessly to your dog's lead like a cocoon.

Imagined and designed by Canberra dog lover Rachel Hawes, the Pupoon helps take care of the whole clean-up job by giving you somewhere airtight and secure to store the poop bags until you can find a rubbish bin.

Winner of an ACT Government innovation grant, the clever all-in-one waste solution takes the ewww out of dog poop disposal, so our footpaths, parks, sporting ovals, suburbs and waterways can e dog-poop free, for everyone to enjoy.

Collar. Lead. Pupoon!

Get yours online at:
Website: www.pupoon.com
Instagram: @thepupoon
Facebook: www.facebook.com/people/Pupoon/61555690354221/

A DogHits Pty Ltd product

GOOD DOG SPONSORS

Camp Bow Wow is a small 5 star boarding kennel operating in Wallaroo which is on the Northern outskirts of Canberra. We focus on maintaining a low-stress environment which dogs adapt to quickly and genuinely enjoy their time with us while their owners are away. We provide premium food, multiple exercise sessions daily, climate-controlled kennels and regular updates to owners. All staff have a genuine love of dogs and we develop strong connections with our returning guests. We also provide weight management services (for both weight loss and weight gain), and post-surgery rehab through controlled exercise sessions.

Contact Details:
- **Website:** www.campbowwow.net.au
- **Facebook:** www.facebook.com/CampBowWowCanberra
- **Location:** 429 Wallaroo Road, Wallaroo NSW 2618

bennetts tax & bas service

Bennetts Tax & BAS Service is a professional tax and accounting firm based in Canberra that specialises in small business taxation, accounting, BAS lodgement, and bookkeeping. Founded and led by Diane, the firm provides tailored financial solutions to help businesses streamline operations, reduce costs, and maximise profitability.

We work with businesses across Australia, offering a hassle-free, secure, and professional service to keep you compliant and financially organised. Whether you're looking for taxation support, business support, or bookkeeping expertise, our team ensures that managing your obligations is simple, transparent, and stress-free.

Contact Details:
- **Email:** admin@bennettstax.com.au
- **Website:** www.bennettstax.com.au
- **Instagram:** @bennetts_tax
- **Phone:** 02 6181 0922
- **Location:** Suite 15, George Turner House, 11 McKay Gardens, Turner 2612

GOOD DOG SPONSORS

Cognitive Canine specialises in walk & train services, focusing on lead-pulling, reactivity, and wrangling energetic breeds like Staffies. Our small team of experienced dog trainers and walkers is dedicated to empowering owners by building stronger bonds with their dogs through effective training and understanding canine communication. We're here to help you and your dog thrive together.

Contact Details
Email: cognitivecaninecanberra@gmail.com
Website: www.cognitivecanine.com.au
Instagram: @cognitivecaninecanberra

CANBERRA PROPERTY PARTNERS

Canberra Property Partners is a trusted local agency dedicated to providing exceptional property management and sales services across the ACT. We pride ourselves on professionalism, transparency, and long-term relationships built on trust. With years of experience managing homes as if they were our own, we deliver a level of care and communication that gives owners complete peace of mind. Beyond real estate, founder, Brett Russell, shares an equal passion for dogs. Whether it's fostering rescues, supporting local shelters, or simply spending weekends with his own four-legged friends, Brett believes dogs bring warmth, loyalty, and joy the same values that inspire how CPP treats every client and every home.

Contact Details
Email: sales@canberrapropertypartners.com.au
Website: www.canberrapropertypartners.com.au
Phone: 02 6103 0843
Location: 2/18 Winchcombe Court, Mitchell ACT 2911

Your Dog's Story. Your Home. Your Heart.

If these pages have made you smile, or tear up a little or hold your dog a bit closer...

Maybe now feels like the right time to create something for your own home.

I offer a personalised photography experience for dogs and the people who adore them.

Relaxed. Pet-led. Full of connection. Every detail is guided with care, so you never wonder "What next?"

We start by getting to know you and your dog. Their quirks. What they love. What you love about them. The little things you want to remember forever.

Then together, we create the photographs into artwork that you'll look at every single day and feel something every single time.

Albums filled with favourite memories. Wall art that makes you smile as you walk past with coffee in hand. Portrait boxes that hold the moments you never want to forget. Beautiful, tangible pieces designed for your home and your heart.

Because digital files live in phones. Artwork lives in your home and your heart.

A Thank-You Gift for Readers

You're here because you love a dog deeply. That's worth celebrating.

As a thank you for supporting this book and Completely Rescue we have a special offer.

Book the Signature Experience $1190 which Includes:
- Your personalised photography session
- $1000 artwork credit
- Get a bonus $500 artwork credit exclusively for *Tails of Canberra Volume 2* readers
- **Total artwork credit: $1500**

When you scan the QR code to book your consultation you'll be asked how you found me. Please write: *Tails of Canberra Volume 2* Book

A limited number of book-reader experiences are available each year so every client receives a premium journey from start to finish.

I'd love to help you celebrate your own best friend.

"Dogs are not our whole life, but they make our lives whole."

Roger Caras

Storyboard collage, framed metal print

Keepsake portrait box

Framed metal wall art

"Everyone thinks they have the best dog. And none of them are wrong."

W. R. Purche

www.ingramcontent.com/pod-product-compliance
Lightning Source LLC
Chambersburg PA
CBRC091747290426
43661CB00134B/1313